MY VERY OWN BOOK OF

ARMS & ARMOR

Designed by

_____

Suit of iron

The main body armor worn by early knights was made of mail, which consisted of thick iron linked together like a chain. As mail was flexible, a heavy blow to the knight could easily cause broken bones or bruising. By the 14th century, armorers invented plate armor to withstand lances, arrows, and swords. A suit of plate armor weighed about 44-55 lb (20-25 kg). The weight was spread over the body so that a fit man could run, lie down, or even mount a horse.

Basinet
This basinet of the late 14th century was originally fitted with a visor that pivoted over the brow. The chain mail guard would have protected the knight's neck.

Chain mail
Mail was easier and cheaper for a blacksmith to make than a complicated suit of plate armor. But it did not give very good protection against enemy weapons.

Fluted gauntlet
Typical of the long, fluted style popular for German "Gothic" armor of the late 15th century, the missing finger and thumb plates would be riveted to a glove attached inside.

Cuisse and poleyn
This is an early 16th-century defense for the thigh and knee of the right leg. The back of the thigh was usually left unprotected.

Italian breastplate
Made by a renowned Italian armorer, this light, strong, one-piece breastplate is a technically perfect piece of plate armor. It is decorated with engraved figures and has a lance-rest for tilting in a joust.

Bird man on parade
A knight would have worn this helmet in a parade at a tournament. Two teams of knights would fight in a joust (mock battle). The defeated knights would have to give up their horses and armor to the victor.

Barbute
A barbute helmet completely enclosed the head. The rivets secured a canvas lining band inside, to which a padded lining was sewn.

Foot-combat headgear
This helmet was worn for foot combat in a tournament. It is so richly gilded that it is surprising that it was ever worn in actual combat.

Quality armor
This ornate German gauntlet is shaped like a fist. It is made from high quality plate armor.

The latest fashion
This breastplate followed the fashion in becoming more and more pointed at the waist until, as here, the full shape known as the "peascod" is formed.

Freedom of movement
A knight's gauntlets were very flexible so he did not have any trouble getting a good grip on his weapons.

Armet
This German armet helmet from around 1535 has a visor that fits inside the rim of the bevor.

Jousting helm
After the 1350s, a helm was worn for tilting. Tilting was charging the opponent when knights tried to unhorse each other with their lances.

Warriors from the East and West

Warriors and knights prided themselves in their expertise in warfare. Throughout history, certain warriors have gained great reputation for their vigor, courage, and aggressiveness on the battlefield. Warriors often underwent rigorous training in the use of weaponry. Both armor and weaponry were quite sophisticated in medieval times, and usually designed with the intention of frightening the enemy.

Buffalo head
A buffalo-horned kabuto would have been worn by a high-ranking samurai officer.

Devil-horned helmet
This Indo-Persian helmet is called a kulah khud. It is adorned with a decorated devil's face, a plume holder, and a pointed spike.

A suit for a samurai
A samurai fought with swords, so armor had to permit free and rapid movement while also providing good protection against a heavy blow. This example of samurai armor is from the 19th century and is called a tosei gusoku.

Handy armor
The Indian vambrace, or dastana, was fastened to the arm with straps. This one is inlaid with gold and silver.

HEADGEAR

A Japanese helmet (kabuto) was secured to the head with cords attached to the brim

A helm was the largest and heaviest helmet a knight ever wore

This Italian barbute resembles an ancient Greek helmet

This Indo-Persian helmet has a mail curtain to protect the eyes and neck

The Germans called this basinet a Hundsgugel (hounds hood)

This gilt bronze helmet belonged to an Anglo-Saxon king called Raedwald

This Spanish morion shows how ornate some 16th-century armor could be

This helmet has a strange, masklike visor in the shape of an eagle's beak

This Celtic warrior helmet was found in the Thames River in London

This imperial German officer's helmet bears the eagle of the rulers of Prussia

HAND WEAPONS

This ceremonial knife from Sudan is called a niam niam

This copper dagger was used by the Kasai people of West Africa

This dagger's handle is inlaid with rubies and diamonds

This tomahawk combines an ax blade with a tobacco pipe

A tanto is a typical samurai dagger

This Indian dagger is called a khanjar

The hollow handle of this tabar (Indian ax) conceals a dagger

Fakir's horns are really a single double-ended dagger with horn grips

In the late 18th century, pistols replaced swords as the preferred method of fighting a duel

This popular weapon of the 1840s and 1850s combined a pistol and pocket knife

The Buntline Special revolver is a long-barreled version of the Colt Peacemaker

This palm pistol, or "lemon squeezer," could be held almost hidden in the hand

A Medieval Knight

The cheek-pieces of this helmet pivot outward

Knights often wore mail or padding beneath their helmet

This helmet was worn during a tournament

A pauldron protected a knight's shoulder

A vambrace protected the upper arm

A knight's breastplate was flared so that sword strokes would bounce off it

Tassets protected the abdomen and upper thighs

Knights did not use daggers until the 14th century

A gauntlet was made of many small pieces so that the hand could move freely

A two-handed sword would deliver a powerful blow

This sword could burst open the links of a piece of mail

A Samurai Warrior

This kabuto
is fitted with
a buffalo-
horn crest

A samurai wore a
mask called a menpo

This kabuto has an opening for
the warrior's pigtail to pass through

Beginning in the
19th century,
Japanese armor
was made
more solid
to provide
protection
from bullets

A sode
protected
a samurai's
shoulder

The mail
on this
armored sleeve
is called kusari

A samurai carried
both short and
long swords

HAND WEAPONS

This Indian battle-ax has a short, heavy, two-edged blade

South American gauchos took part in knife duels

Archers often sheltered behind a large shield when firing weapons

The sheath of this Chinese sword is made of tortoiseshell

This Malay dagger has a wavy blade

A tribal chief from the Iron Age owned this dagger

The hilt of this Sudanese dagger is decorated with beaten silver coins

This is an early type of bayonet called a plug bayonet

An Indian or Persian warrior would hold this round shield in the left arm

This stabbing ax was used by the Matabele people of Zimbabwe

A plume of animal hair hangs from this war ax

The blade of this Spanish knife folds back to sit partly within the hilt

Early ax heads were made of stone or bronze

Body Armor

A gauntlet was riveted to the back of a leather glove

A samurai haidate (thigh defense) was made of silk

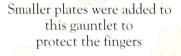

Smaller plates were added to this gauntlet to protect the fingers

This mail shirt is made from solid iron rings

An Indian breastplate was known as a char aina

This breastplate resembles a 16th-century doublet (close-fitting jacket)

This vambrace (for the lower arm) has a chain mail extension for the hand

A samurai greave is called a suneate

This gauntlet was made in northern Germany

Rivets in plate armor allowed a knight to bend

This fluted gauntlet is made from plate armor

A sabaton (foot armor) had to be very flexible

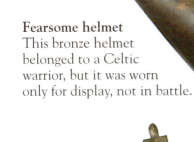

Fearsome helmet
This bronze helmet belonged to a Celtic warrior, but it was worn only for display, not in battle.

Rectangular breastplate
The char aina has mail shoulder straps with metal clasps and would have been worn over a mail shirt.

Samurai dagger
High-quality steel was used to make samurai weapons. It took many hours to produce such fine weapons.

Changing styles
Japanese helmets developed from prehistoric times through to the 19th century. Helmets from each period had their own styles and features.

Suneate
A greave was tied to the leg with colored silk. The inside was lined with fabric.

Warrior king
King Raedwald was an able warrior, a necessity for a leader in warlike early Anglo-Saxon society.

Recurved dagger
Many Indian weapons were remarkably similar to those used by Persian and Turkish warriors.

In combat

People have always used weapons to hunt, attack others, and to defend themselves.

The discovery of metals such as copper and bronze revolutionized the making of hand held weapons. With the invention of gunpowder, long-range warfare replaced hand-to-hand combat when cannonballs and bullets were launched onto the battlefield.

Simple but deadly
The first weapons were ax-heads made of stone or bronze. With the invention of the handle, prehistoric people found that hunting and attacking weapons were more reliable and much stronger.

An affair of honor
Dueling used to be a popular way for gentlemen and army officers to settle their quarrels. Two duelers would stand a number of paces apart. At a given signal, the duelers raised their pistols and fired.

What a shot!
In the 19th century, a great variety of pistols were designed for both military and civilian use. Some could only fire a single shot – but a revolver could fire a succession of shots before it needed reloading.

Stabbing ax
As the handle is angled in line with the pointed end of the blade, this ax can be used for a stabbing and a chopping action.

Folding knife
The blade of this Spanish folding knife was locked in place by a steel spring in the hilt.

Symbol of honor
The swords used by samurai warriors were some of the finest swords ever made. Learning to use the sword correctly took years of hard work – there were many moves that the warrior had to perfect.

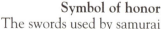

War mask
A samurai warrior war mask was called a menpo. It gave the wearer a frightening appearance to alarm the enemy.

Oriental sword
The military success of China was displayed in fine weapons, such as swords and daggers.

All-steel battle-ax
This Indian battle-ax is called a tabar. It has an extended blade with a slightly rounded cutting edge.

Circular shield
In the 18th century, both Indian and Persian soldiers used a round shield, called a dhal or sipar, made of steel or hide.

Sudanese dagger
Of Arabian origin, this dagger is used for both war and ceremony in the Middle East and India.

Iron-Age dagger
The bronze sheath of this dagger would have hung from a chieftain's belt by iron hoops.

Armor piercer
A pesh-kabz was a dagger, specially made to pierce mail. The blade was wide at the hilt, narrowing to a cutting edge before tapering to a sharp point.

Apache tomahawk pipe
Before Native Americans were supplied iron by European traders, they made their tomahawk heads with stone.

Bizarre hand weapons

Throughout history quite extraordinary weapons have been made alongside conventional swords, guns, bows, and arrows. Many ancient weapons were equally as inventive and deadly as modern weapons specially designed for close-range attack and defense. Unusual pistols were often custom-made by gunsmiths for wealthy customers, too.

Assassin's pistol
This handheld pistol was fired using a squeezing action. One was used to assassinate US President William McKinley.

Deadly combination
This weapon includes a pistol, two knife blades, a ramrod, and space in the grip for ammunition.

Tickled to death
The dao is an impressive looking war-ax from Assam, in India. It would have been used during intertribal warfare.

Spiky horns
Fakir's horns were used as a defensive weapon by fakirs. These Hindu holy men were not allowed to carry ordinary weapons because of their religion.

Bayonet
Early bayonets were knives or daggers inserted into the muzzle of a musket for use as a secondary weapon.

Golden elephant
Known as a bhuj, this knifelike battle-ax from northern India is also called an "elephant head" because it has a carving of an elephant head between the shaft and blade.